Autographs

B IS FOR Broadway

Onstage and Backstage from A to Z

Written by
John Robert Allman

Illustrated by
Peter Emmerich

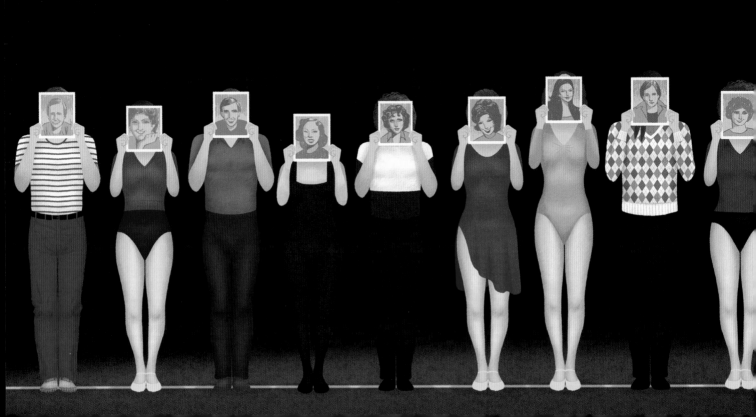

A is for auditions, at which actors try their best. A *Chorus Line* puts dazzling, driven dancers to the test.

B is for backstage, abuzz with bustling cast and crew.
Look out for curtains, chandeliers, and costumes coming through!

Jerome Robbins (front) and Sharks, *West Side Story*, 1957

C's for choreographers, who dramatize with dances,
from Mr. Robbins's rumbles to Ms. Stroman's sweet romances.

Deborah Yates as Girl in a Yellow Dress and Susan Stroman, *Contact*, 2000

D is for directors and designers, whose decisions can ensure a show is smashing and as vibrant as their visions.

EXIT

Jennifer Holliday as Effie White, Michael Bennett, Theoni V. Aldredge, Tharon Musser,
and Robin Wagner, *Dreamgirls*, 1981

E is for ensemble, or the singing, dancing chorus.
In *42nd Street*, their thrilling tapping talents floor us.

Ensemble, *42nd Street*, 1980

F is for finales
that make second acts complete.
Watch Tracy shake and shimmy,
singing "You Can't Stop the Beat."

Matthew Morrison (in white) as Link Larkin, Marissa Jaret Winokur (in pink polka dots) as Tracy Turnblad, Kerry Butler (in purple) as Penny Pingleton, Mary Bond Davis (in yellow) as Motormouth Maybelle, Harvey Fierstein (in red) as Edna Turnblad, and ensemble, *Hairspray*, 2002

RICHARD RODGERS

ST. JAMES

ROYALE

MINSKOFF THEATRE

N

NEDERLANDER

SHUBERT

Winter Garden

Barrymore

GOLDEN

Cort

IMPERIAL

Music Box

G is for the glitter and
the glow of Broadway's lights
on the magical marquees
that beam on brilliant opening nights.

His hits like *Hamilton*, which crowds and critics cheer.
A smash like *Rent* or *Wicked* sells out year to year to year.

Daveed Diggs as Thomas Jefferson, Lin-Manuel Miranda as Alexander Hamilton, and Leslie Odom, Jr., as Aaron Burr, *Hamilton*, 2015

(Back row, L to R) Adam Pascal as Roger Davis, Daphne Rubin-Vega as Mimi Marquez, and Anthony Rapp as Mark Cohen, *Rent*, 1996 | (Front row, L to R) Kristin Chenoweth as Glinda and Idina Menzel as Elphaba, *Wicked*, 200?

I's for intermission, or the break between the acts
for perusing *Playbill*, scoring souvenirs, or snagging snacks.

(Back row, L to R) Phylicia Rashad, Debbie Allen, Tommy Tune, and Sarah Jessica Parker |
(Front row, L to R) Harold Prince and George C. Wolfe

is for the jazz hands that were favorite moves of Fosse's
for *Chicago* and *Sweet Charity* and *Pippin*'s playful posses.

K is for those killer kick lines musicals provide.
See Liza and her chorus kicking side by side by side.

Liza Minnelli as Michelle Craig and ensemble, *The Act*, 1977

(Back row, L to R) Angela Lansbury as Mame Dennis, *Mame*, 1966 | Chita Rivera as Spider Woman/Aurora, *Kiss of the Spider Woman*, 1993 | Zero Mostel as Tevye, *Fiddler on the Roof*, 1964 | Patti LuPone as Reno Sweeney, *Anything Goes*, 1987 | (Middle row, L to R) Ethel Waters, *As Thousands Cheer*, 1933 | Nathan Lane and Matthew Broderick as Max Bialystock and Leo Bloom, *The Producers*, 2001 | Ruby Dee and Sidney Poitier as Ruth Younger and Walter Lee Younger, *A Raisin in the Sun*, 1959 |

L is for the leading men and ladies fans adore, whose powerhouse performances leave patrons wanting more.

(Front row, L to R) Barbra Streisand as Fanny Brice, *Funny Girl*, 1964 | Audra McDonald as Sharon, *Master Class*, 1995 | Marlon Brando and Jessica Tandy as Stanley Kowalski and Blanche DuBois, *A Streetcar Named Desire*, 1947 | Robert Preston as Harold Hill, *The Music Man*, 1957 | Billy Porter as Lola, *Kinky Boots*, 2013 | Mary Martin as Maria Rainer, *The Sound of Music*, 1959 | John Raitt as Billy Bigelow, *Carousel*, 1945 | Joel Grey as Master of Ceremonies, *Cabaret*, 1966

M is for the makeup used for flawless feline faces
before the cast of *Cats* is set to scamper to their places.

Hello, Dolly! at the Orpheum Theatre, Minneapolis, 1965

MARY MARTIN IN "HELLO, DOLLY!"

N is for the national tours
that share New York's sensations
with cities round the country,
where they're welcomed with ovations.

O is for the orchestras that skillfully play scores
as they follow their conductors' lead from under stages' floors.

P is for the playwrights who write poignant, potent plays, their comedies and dramas met with prizes and with praise.

(Top row, L to R) Tony Kushner, Edward Albee, August Wilson, and Arthur Miller | (Middle row, L to R) Lorraine Hansberry, Tennessee Williams, Neil Simon, and Eugene O'Neill | (Bottom row, L to R) Lillian Hellman, Terrence McNally, and Wendy Wasserstein

Bernadette Peters as the Witch, *Into the Woods*, 1987

Q is for a quick change, which can help an actress switch
to a stunner within seconds from a wrinkly, wicked witch.

Betty Garde as Aunt Eller and Alfred Drake as Curly, *Oklahoma!*, 1943

R is for revivals, which, when daringly directed,
can revitalize a show in ways unique and unexpected.

Ali Stroker as Ado Annie and Mary Testa as Aunt Eller, *Oklahoma!*, 2019

S is for the songwriters, whose stirring, soaring tunes
are what Henry Higgins bellows and what Dolly Levi croons.

(Back row, L to R) Leonard Bernstein, Adolph Green, Betty Comden, Richard Rodgers, Alan Jay Lerner, Frederick Loewe, Oscar Hammerstein II, Jerry Herman, Eubie Blake, and Jeanine Tesori | (Seated left, L to R) Stephen Sondheim and George Gershwin | (Seated right, L to R) Cole Porter and Andrew Lloyd Webber | (Front) Irving Berlin

Rosie O'Donnell, Hugh Jackman, Neil Patrick Harris, and Gregory Hines

T is for the Tony, which is short for Antoinette.
Every June, the best of Broadway win the spinning statuette.

U's for understudies, who swoop in if there's a sprain.
"At this performance, Gladys will be played by Ms. MacLaine."

Shirley MacLaine as Gladys and dancers, *The Pajama Game*, 1954

V is for the vocals
that can reach the mezzanine,
whether Adelaide and Nathan
or the Phantom and Christine.

Vivian Blaine as Miss Adelaide and Sam Levene as Nathan Detroit, *Guys and Dolls*, 1950 | Sarah Brightman as
Christine Daaé and Michael Crawford as the Phantom of the Opera, *The Phantom of the Opera*, 1988

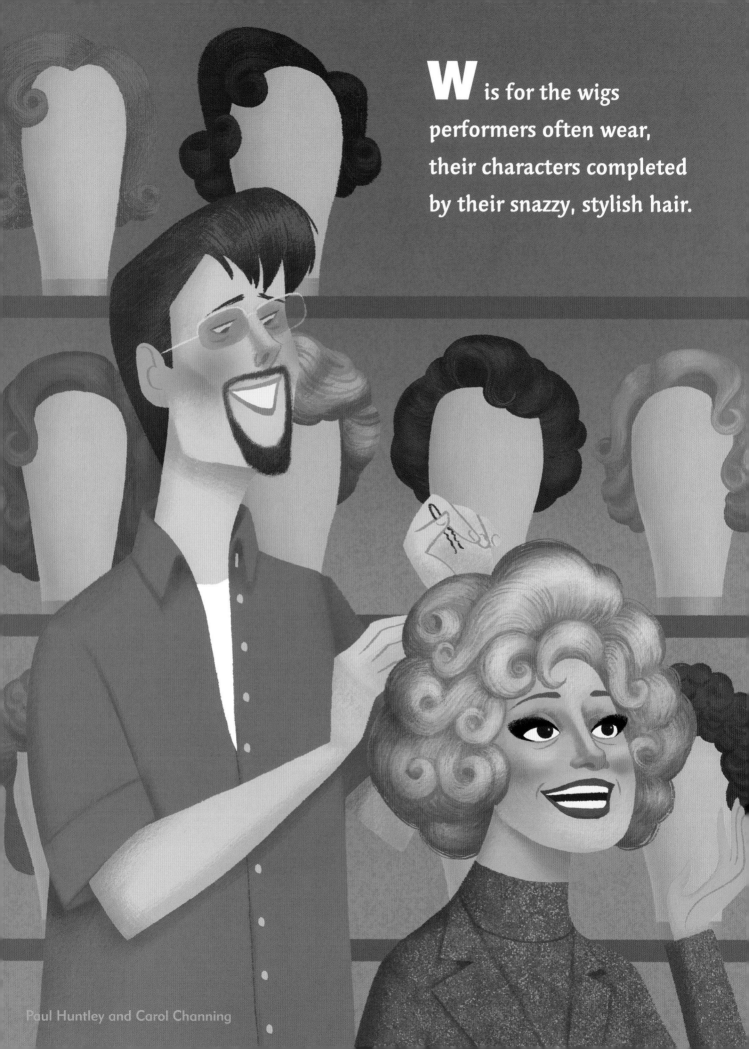

W is for the wigs
performers often wear,
their characters completed
by their snazzy, stylish hair.

Paul Huntley and Carol Channing

X is for the X-shaped spikes that stagehands stick to stages so that Stokes is sure of where to stand as Don Quixote rages.

Brian Stokes Mitchell as Don Quixote (Cervantes), *Man of La Mancha*, 2002

Y is for the youngest stars to stun with song-and-dancin' as optimistic Annie or as anxious Evan Hansen.

(Back row, L to R) Bruce Prochnik as Oliver Twist, *Oliver!*, 1963 | Andrea McArdle as Annie, *Annie*, 1977 |
Daisy Eagan as Mary Lennox, *The Secret Garden*, 1991 | Sydney Lucas as Small Alison, *Fun Home*, 2015 |
Stephanie Mills as Dorothy, *The Wiz*, 1975 | David Alvarez as Billy Elliot, *Billy Elliot: The Musical*, 2008

(Front row, L to R) Baayork Lee as Princess Ying Yaowalak, *The King and I*, 1951 | Alfonso Ribeiro as Willie, *The Tap Dance Kid*, 1983 | Oona Laurence as Matilda, *Matilda: The Musical*, 2013 | Ben Platt as Evan Hansen, *Dear Evan Hansen*, 2016

Z's for Mr. Ziegfeld and producers who invest in provocative productions penned by some of Broadway's best.

Florenz Ziegfeld, Jr., *Show Boat*, 1927

From A to Z, you know the showbiz slang you've got to know.
So, as Ethel Merman belted out, let's go on with the show!

Ethel Merman as Mrs. Sally Adams, *Call Me Madam*, 1950

EDWARD ALBEE wrote many groundbreaking plays, including *Who's Afraid of Virginia Woolf?* (1962) and *The Goat, or Who Is Sylvia?* (2002), both of which won Tony Awards for Best Play. He also received three Pulitzer Prizes for Drama, a Special Tony Award for Lifetime Achievement, a Kennedy Center Honor, and the National Medal of Arts.

THEONI V. ALDREDGE was a costume designer whose career spanned over four decades. She won three Tony Awards—for *Annie* (1977), *Barnum* (1980), and *La Cage aux Folles* (1983)—as well as an Academy Award for *The Great Gatsby*.

DEBBIE ALLEN is an Emmy Award–winning and Tony Award–nominated performer, director, and choreographer, beloved as Lydia Grant in *Fame*. She debuted on Broadway in *Purlie* (1970) before starring in shows including *West Side Story* (1980) and *Sweet Charity* (1986), choreographing *Carrie* (1988), and directing *Cat on a Hot Tin Roof* (2008). In 2020, she was named a Kennedy Center Honoree.

DAVID ALVAREZ originated the title role in *Billy Elliot: The Musical* (2008) on Broadway alongside Kiril Kulish and Trent Kowalik. All three won Tony Awards for their performances.

RENEE BAUGHMAN made her Broadway debut in *Applause* (1970) before creating the role of Kristine in *A Chorus Line* (1975).

MICHAEL BENNETT was a director-choreographer best known for conceiving, directing, and co-choreographing *A Chorus Line* (1975), for which he won two of his seven Tonys and a Pulitzer Prize. He was also director, choreographer, or both for *Promises, Promises* (1968), *Company* (1970), *Follies* (1971), and *Dreamgirls* (1981).

IRVING BERLIN was a prolific songwriter whose hit tunes included "Blue Skies," "God Bless America," and, from *Annie Get Your Gun*, "There's No Business Like Show Business." He won an Oscar for "White Christmas" and a Tony for *Call Me Madam* (1950) as well as two Special Tonys, a Grammy for Lifetime Achievement, and the Presidential Medal of Freedom.

LEONARD BERNSTEIN was a composer, conductor, and pianist whose work spanned theater, ballet, and film as well as symphonic, chamber, and choral music. His scores for Broadway include *On the Town* (1944), *Wonderful Town* (1953), for which he won a Tony Award, *Candide* (1956), and *West Side Story* (1957). He served as music director of the New York Philharmonic for eleven seasons and was the recipient of a Special Tony, seventeen Grammys, eleven Emmys, and a Kennedy Center Honor.

KELLY BISHOP won the Tony Award for Best Featured Actress in a Musical for her turn as Sheila in *A Chorus Line* (1975). She later played Emily Gilmore on TV's *Gilmore Girls*.

VIVIAN BLAINE was a film, television, and theater actress best known for creating the role of Miss Adelaide in *Guys and Dolls* (1950), on stage and in the film.

PAMELA BLAIR played Val in *A Chorus Line* (1975). Her Broadway credits also include *Promises, Promises* (1968) and *Seesaw* (1973).

EUBIE BLAKE was a songwriter who, with collaborator Noble Sissle, scored *Shuffle Along* (1921), which introduced "I'm Just Wild About Harry" and was among the first Broadway musicals to be helmed by an African American creative team. His music inspired the Broadway revue *Eubie!* (1978), for which he was nominated for a Tony, and in 1981, he received the Presidential Medal of Freedom.

MARLON BRANDO was a two-time Academy Award–winning actor who originated the role of Stanley Kowalski in *A Streetcar Named Desire* (1947), both on Broadway and in the film.

SARAH BRIGHTMAN is a Grammy-nominated vocalist who has performed in West End and Broadway musicals including *The Phantom of the Opera* (1988) and *Aspects of Love* (1990).

MATTHEW BRODERICK is a three-time Tony Award–nominated actor and two-time winner, for *Brighton Beach Memoirs* (1983) and *How to Succeed in Business Without Really Trying* (1995). He starred opposite Nathan Lane in *The Producers* (2001) on stage and screen.

KERRY BUTLER originated the roles of Penny in *Hairspray* (2002); Clio/Kira in *Xanadu* (2007), for which she was nominated for a Tony Award; and Barbara in *Beetlejuice* (2019).

CAROL CHANNING starred in *Gentlemen Prefer Blondes* (1949) before originating her Tony Award–winning role, Dolly Levi in *Hello, Dolly!* (1964). She also received two Special Tony Awards, including one for Lifetime Achievement.

KRISTIN CHENOWETH won a Tony Award for her breakout performance as Sally in *You're a Good Man, Charlie Brown* (1999). She has since garnered nominations for *Wicked* (2003) and *On the Twentieth Century* (2015), and won an Emmy Award for *Pushing Daisies*.

WAYNE CILENTO created the role of Mike in *A Chorus Line* (1975) and later turned to choreography. He has been nominated for seven Tony Awards, winning for Best Choreography for *The Who's Tommy* (1993).

KAY COLE made her Broadway debut in *Bye Bye Birdie* (1960) and appeared in shows including *Hair* (1968) and *Jesus Christ Superstar* (1971) before playing Maggie in *A Chorus Line* (1975).

BETTY COMDEN was half of a lyric, libretto, and screenwriting duo with Adolph Green. Their work included the book and lyrics for *On the Town* (1944), the lyrics for *The Will Rogers Follies* (1991), and the screenplay for *Singin' in the Rain,* which later became a Broadway musical. Over the course of their six-decade partnership, they were nominated for two Academy Awards and seven Tony Awards, winning four.

MICHAEL CRAWFORD created the role of the Phantom in *The Phantom of the Opera* (1988) in the West End and on Broadway, winning both a Tony and his second Olivier Award.

MARY BOND DAVIS's Broadway credits include *Jelly's Last Jam* (1992) and *Hairspray* (2002), in which she originated the role of Motormouth Maybelle.

RUBY DEE was an Emmy and Grammy Award–winning actress, writer, and activist who originated the role of Ruth Younger in *A Raisin in the Sun* (1959) on stage and screen. She was nominated for an Oscar for *American Gangster,* received the National Medal of Arts, and was a Kennedy Center Honoree.

RONALD DENNIS first appeared on Broadway in the Pearl Bailey–led company of *Hello, Dolly!* (1967) before playing Richie in *A Chorus Line* (1975).

DAVEED DIGGS won Tony and Grammy Awards for his performances as Marquis de Lafayette and Thomas Jefferson in *Hamilton* (2015).

ALFRED DRAKE was a two-time Tony Award recipient, including a Special Tony Honor for Excellence in Theatre. His credits include *Oklahoma!* (1943), *Kiss Me, Kate* (1948), and *Kismet* (1953).

DAISY EAGAN won the Tony Award for Best Featured Actress in a Musical at age eleven for her turn as Mary Lennox in *The Secret Garden* (1991).

HARVEY FIERSTEIN is a four-time Tony Award–winning actor, playwright, and librettist, winning for both Best Play and Best Actor in a Play for *Torch Song Trilogy* (1982), for Best Book for *La Cage aux Folles* (1983), and for Best Actor in a Musical for *Hairspray* (2002), in which he created the role of Edna Turnblad.

BOB FOSSE was a dancer, director, and choreographer whose shows include *The Pajama Game* (1954), *Sweet Charity* (1966), and *Chicago* (1975). He won nine Tony Awards, three Emmys, and an Oscar.

BETTY GARDE was an actress who is best remembered for originating the role of Aunt Eller in *Oklahoma!* (1943).

TRISH GARLAND originated the role of Judy in *A Chorus Line* (1975), having previously danced in *Follies* (1971).

PAUL GEMIGNANI is an Emmy-winning and Grammy-nominated music director and conductor who has worked on forty Broadway shows, including a dozen with Stephen Sondheim. In 2001, he received a Special Tony Award for Lifetime Achievement.

GEORGE GERSHWIN was a celebrated composer who worked across theater, opera, film, and orchestral music. His collaboration with his brother, lyricist Ira Gershwin, produced some of Broadway's most iconic songs, including "Summertime" from *Porgy and Bess* (1935). His best-known compositions include *Rhapsody in Blue* and *An American in Paris*. He was posthumously nominated for an Academy Award for Best Song for *Shall We Dance*.

ADOLPH GREEN and his writing partner, Betty Comden, wrote lyrics, librettos, and screenplays together for over sixty years. Their acclaimed work earned them seven Tony nominations and four wins, including two, for Best Book and Score, for *On the Twentieth Century* (1978). They were nominated twice for an Academy Award.

JOEL GREY is an actor and director whose career has spanned seven decades. He created the role of the Master of Ceremonies in *Cabaret* (1966), for which he won a Tony Award, as well as an Oscar for the film. His stage credits include *Chicago* (1996) and *Wicked* (2003).

OSCAR HAMMERSTEIN II was a Tony, Oscar, Grammy, and Pulitzer-winning lyricist, librettist, and producer whose book and lyrics for *Show Boat* (1927) helped break new ground in American musical theater. His legendary collaborations with composer Richard Rodgers included *Oklahoma!* (1943), *Carousel* (1945), *South Pacific* (1949), *The King and I* (1951), and *The Sound of Music* (1959).

LORRAINE HANSBERRY was the first Black female dramatist to have a play produced on Broadway, *A Raisin in the Sun* (1959), for which she was nominated for a Tony Award.

NEIL PATRICK HARRIS won the Tony Award for Best Actor in a Musical for *Hedwig and the Angry Inch* (2014). He also won four Emmys for his stints as host of the Tony Awards.

LILLIAN HELLMAN was a writer, playwright, and screenwriter whose numerous Broadway plays include *The Children's Hour* (1934) and *The Little Foxes* (1939). She was nominated for two Tony Awards, for *Candide* (1956) and *Toys in the Attic* (1960).

JERRY HERMAN was a composer-lyricist known for his showtune-stuffed scores for musicals including *Hello, Dolly!* (1964), *Mame* (1966), *Mack and Mabel* (1974), and *La Cage aux Folles* (1983). He was the recipient of two Tonys for Best Score and a Special Tony for Lifetime Achievement, as well as two Grammys and a Kennedy Center Honor.

GREGORY HINES, a two-time Tony Awards co-host, was an actor, singer, dancer, and choreographer. He was nominated for five Tonys, winning for Best Actor in a Musical for *Jelly's Last Jam* (1992), for which he also provided tap choreography.

JENNIFER HOLLIDAY is an actress and recording artist who won a Tony Award for her turn as Effie White in *Dreamgirls* (1981).

PAUL HUNTLEY has designed hair and wigs for hundreds of Broadway shows, including *Amadeus* (1980), *Cats* (1982), *The Producers* (2001), and *Hairspray* (2002). He was awarded a Special Tony Honor for Excellence in Theatre in 2003.

HUGH JACKMAN won the Tony Award for Best Actor in a Musical for *The Boy from Oz* (2003), his Broadway debut, and also received a Special Tony. He has hosted the Tony Awards four times and won an Emmy for the 2005 telecast.

RON KUHLMAN created the role of Don in *A Chorus Line* (1975) and, like many in the cast, played the role again on the show's first national tour.

TONY KUSHNER is an award-winning playwright and screenwriter. His two-part play, *Angels in America* (1993), earned him a Pulitzer Prize, two Tonys, and an Emmy for its television adaptation. He is also a recipient of the National Medal of Arts.

NANCY LANE made her Broadway debut as Bebe in *A Chorus Line* (1975), having previously toured in 1973's *Seesaw*.

NATHAN LANE is a six-time Tony Award–nominated actor and three-time winner for his performances as Pseudolus in *A Funny Thing Happened on the Way to the Forum* (1996), Max Bialystock in *The Producers* (2001), and Roy Cohn in *Angels in America* (2018).

ANGELA LANSBURY has been nominated for seven Tony Awards, winning five times for her roles in *Mame* (1966), *Dear World* (1969), *Gypsy* (1974), *Sweeney Todd* (1979), and *Blithe Spirit* (2009). She has received three Oscar nominations and earned twelve Emmy nominations for *Murder, She Wrote*.

OONA LAURENCE is one of four actresses to originate the role of Matilda in *Matilda: The Musical* (2013) on Broadway. She, Sophia Gennusa, Bailey Ryon, and Milly Shapiro received Special Tony Honors for Excellence in Theatre for their performances.

BAAYORK LEE performed in ten Broadway shows, including *The King and I* (1951), before creating the role of Connie in *A Chorus Line* (1975), for which she was also the dance captain and assistant to the choreographers. In 2017, Lee received the Tony Awards' Isabelle Stevenson Award for her work as a cofounder of National Asian Artists Project.

ALAN JAY LERNER was a lyricist and librettist best known for his storied successes with composer Frederick Loewe. Their Broadway hits included *Brigadoon* (1947), *My Fair Lady* (1956), *Camelot* (1960), and *Gigi* (1973). Lerner's accolades include three Tony Awards, three Academy Awards, and a Kennedy Center Honor.

SAM LEVENE was a Tony-nominated actor, for *The Devil's Advocate* (1961), whose other Broadway credits included Nathan in *Guys and Dolls* (1950) and Al in *The Sunshine Boys* (1972).

FREDERICK LOEWE was a composer and two-time Tony Award winner. Alongside lyricist-librettist Alan Jay Lerner, he scored Broadway classics including *Brigadoon* (1947), *My Fair Lady* (1956), *Camelot* (1960), and *Gigi* (1973).

PRISCILLA LOPEZ was nominated for a Tony for her performance as Diana in *A Chorus Line* (1975) and won for *A Day in Hollywood / A Night in the Ukraine* (1980). Her other Broadway shows include *Pippin* (1972 and 2013) and *In the Heights* (2008).

SYDNEY LUCAS created the role of Small Alison in *Fun Home* (2015), earning a Tony nomination at age eleven.

PATTI LuPONE is a seven-time Tony Award nominee and two-time winner, for *Evita* (1979) and *Gypsy* (2008). In London, she originated the roles of Fantine in *Les Misérables* (1985), for which she won the first of two Olivier Awards, and Norma Desmond in *Sunset Boulevard* (1994).

SHIRLEY MacLAINE's "big break" came as an understudy for Carol Haney in *The Pajama Game* (1954). Her subsequent, prolific film work includes *The Apartment, Sweet Charity,* and *Terms of Endearment,* for which she won the Academy Award for Best Actress.

TERRENCE MANN is a three-time Tony Award–nominated actor whose many Broadway credits include Rum Tum Tugger in *Cats* (1982), Javert in *Les Misérables* (1987), and the Beast in *Beauty and the Beast* (1994).

MARY MARTIN originated the legendary roles Ensign Nellie Forbush in *South Pacific* (1949), Peter Pan in *Peter Pan* (1954), and Maria Rainer in *The Sound of Music* (1959), winning Tony Awards for all three. She also received a Special Tony Award in 1948 and headlined the first national tour of *Hello, Dolly!* (1965).

CAMERON MASON made his Broadway debut in *The Pajama Game* (1973) before creating the role of Mark in *A Chorus Line* (1975).

ANDREA McARDLE made her Broadway debut in the title role in *Annie* (1977) at age thirteen, for which she received a Tony nomination.

AUDRA McDONALD has won six competitive Tony Awards—more than any other performer—for her roles in *Carousel* (1994), *Master Class* (1995), *Ragtime* (1998), *A Raisin in the Sun* (2004), *Porgy and Bess* (2012), and *Lady Day at Emerson's Bar & Grill* (2014).

DONNA McKECHNIE first danced on Broadway in *How to Succeed in Business Without Really Trying* (1961). Her other credits include *Promises, Promises* (1968), *Company* (1970), and *A Chorus Line* (1975), for which she won the Tony Award for Best Actress in a Musical for her role as Cassie.

TERRENCE McNALLY was a playwright, librettist, and screenwriter who won four Tonys, for *Kiss of the Spider Woman* (1993), *Love! Valour! Compassion!* (1995), *Master Class* (1995), and *Ragtime* (1998). He was awarded a Special Tony Award for Lifetime Achievement in 2019.

IDINA MENZEL made her Broadway debut in *Rent* (1996), won a Tony Award for her performance as Elphaba in *Wicked* (2003), and introduced the character Elsa in the movie *Frozen*.

ETHEL MERMAN's legendary career included star turns in the original productions of *Anything Goes* (1934); *Annie Get Your Gun* (1946); *Call Me Madam* (1950), for which she won a Tony Award; and *Gypsy* (1959). She was honored with a Special Tony Award in 1972.

ARTHUR MILLER penned three Tony Award–winning Best Plays: *All My Sons* (1947); *Death of a Salesman* (1949), for which he also won the Pulitzer Prize; and *The Crucible* (1953). He also received two Emmy Awards, a Kennedy Center Honor, the National Medal of Arts, and a Special Tony Award for Lifetime Achievement.

PATINA MILLER headlined *Sister Act* (2011) and won a Tony Award for her turn as the Leading Player in *Pippin* (2013).

STEPHANIE MILLS is a Grammy Award–winning recording artist and actress, best known to theater audiences as Dorothy in *The Wiz* (1975).

LIZA MINNELLI won Tony Awards for her Broadway debut at the age of nineteen in *Flora, the Red Menace* (1965) and for *The Act* (1977), as well as a Special Tony Award for "adding lustre to the Broadway season" with her concert engagement *Liza* (1974). She also won an Emmy Award for the special *Liza with a "Z,"* an Oscar for the film *Cabaret,* and a Grammy Legend Award.

LIN-MANUEL MIRANDA is the creator of the Tony Award–winning Best Musicals *In the Heights* (2008) and *Hamilton* (2015), in which he starred as Usnavi and Alexander Hamilton, respectively. As an actor and writer across theater, television, and film, Miranda has received a Pulitzer Prize, three Tony Awards, three Grammy Awards, an Emmy Award, and an Academy Award nomination.

BRIAN STOKES MITCHELL's Broadway acting credits include *Ragtime* (1998), *Kiss Me, Kate* (1999), and *Man of La Mancha* (2002). He has served as Board Chair of The Actors Fund since 2004 and was awarded the Tonys' Isabelle Stevenson Award for his support of the organization in 2016.

MATTHEW MORRISON has acted in Broadway productions including *Hairspray* (2002) and *The Light in the Piazza* (2005), for which he was nominated for a Tony Award.

ZERO MOSTEL was a three-time Tony Award–winning actor who originated roles including Pseudolus in *A Funny Thing Happened on the Way to the Forum* (1962) and Tevye in *Fiddler on the Roof* (1964). He created the role of Max Bialystock in the original film version of *The Producers*.

THARON MUSSER was a pioneering lighting designer whose work on over 150 Broadway shows earned her ten Tony Award nominations and three wins, for *Follies* (1971), *A Chorus Line* (1975), and *Dreamgirls* (1981).

BEBE NEUWIRTH is a dancer, singer, actress, and winner of two Tony Awards, for *Sweet Charity* (1986) and *Chicago* (1996), and two Emmys, for her performance as Dr. Lilith Sternin on *Cheers.* She is Vice Chair of The Actors Fund.

LESLIE ODOM, JR., made his Broadway debut in *Rent* (1996) before winning Tony and Grammy Awards for his star turn as Aaron Burr in *Hamilton* (2015).

ROSIE O'DONNELL's work on Broadway includes starring in *Grease* (1994) and producing *Taboo* (2003). She received the Tonys' Isabelle Stevenson Award in 2014 for her commitment to arts education through Rosie's Theater Kids. She has hosted the Tony Awards three times, winning an Emmy for the 1998 ceremony.

EUGENE O'NEILL was a groundbreaking playwright who won the Nobel Prize in Literature and four Pulitzer Prizes for Drama. His best-known work includes *The Iceman Cometh* (1946), *Long Day's Journey Into Night* (1956), and *A Moon for the Misbegotten* (1957).

CYNTHIA ONRUBIA is a dancer and choreographer who created the role of Victoria in *Cats* (1982) and performed in shows including *A Chorus Line* (1975) and *Dancin'* (1978).

SARAH JESSICA PARKER made her Broadway debut at age eleven in *The Innocents* (1976) before replacing Andrea McArdle in the title role in *Annie* in 1979. She has since worked extensively in film, on television, and on stage.

ADAM PASCAL made his Broadway debut and was nominated for a Tony Award for his performance as Roger in *Rent* (1996).

DON PERCASSI appeared in six Broadway musicals before originating the role of Al in *A Chorus Line* (1975) and later dancing in the original company of *42nd Street* (1980).

BERNADETTE PETERS has been a musical theater mainstay for six decades and has won two Tony Awards, for *Song and Dance* (1985) and *Annie Get Your Gun* (1999). She also received the Tony Awards' Isabelle Stevenson Award for her charitable work as a cofounder of Broadway Barks. In addition to film and television work, her notable theater credits include *Sunday in the Park with George* (1984), *Into the Woods* (1987), and *Gypsy* (2003).

BEN PLATT made his Broadway debut in *The Book of Mormon* (2011) before winning the Tony Award for originating the title role in *Dear Evan Hansen* (2016).

SIDNEY POITIER is an actor, activist, and ambassador and the recipient of a Kennedy Center Honor and the Presidential Medal of Freedom. He created the role of Walter Lee Younger in *A Raisin in the Sun* (1959), for which he was nominated for a Tony. He was the first Black actor to be nominated for an Academy Award for Best Actor, for *The Defiant Ones,* and the first to win, for *Lilies of the Field*.

BILLY PORTER won Tony and Grammy Awards for his star turn as Lola in *Kinky Boots* (2013), and an Emmy Award for his role as Pray Tell on *Pose*. His other Broadway credits include *Grease* (1994) and *Shuffle Along* (2016).

COLE PORTER was a composer-lyricist whose scores for shows spawned numerous standards including "I Get a Kick Out of You" and "You're the Top" from *Anything Goes* (1934). He won a Tony Award for Best Original Score for *Kiss Me, Kate* (1948).

ROBERT PRESTON was a prolific actor in film and theater, best known for creating the role of Harold Hill in *The Music Man* (1957), for which he won the first of his two Tony Awards. He was nominated for an Oscar for his performance in *Victor/Victoria*.

HAROLD PRINCE was a prolific producer and director for over sixty years, receiving twenty-one Tony Awards, a Kennedy Center Honor, and the National Medal of Arts. Among his hits were, as producer, *The Pajama Game* (1954), *West Side Story* (1957), and *Fiddler on the Roof* (1964); as producer-director, *Cabaret* (1966), *Company* (1970), and *A Little Night Music* (1973); and as director, *Evita* (1979), *The Phantom of the Opera* (1988), and *Kiss of the Spider Woman* (1993).

BRUCE PROCHNIK starred as Oliver Twist in the original Broadway production of *Oliver!* (1963) at the age of fourteen.

JOHN RAITT was an actor and singer who lent his baritone to classic roles including Billy Bigelow in *Carousel* (1945) and Sid Sorokin in *The Pajama Game* (1954).

ANTHONY RAPP's Broadway appearances include Mark in *Rent* (1996) and the title role in *You're a Good Man, Charlie Brown* (1999).

PHYLICIA RASHAD is a performer and director whose Broadway performance credits include *The Wiz* (1975), *Dreamgirls* (1981), *Into the Woods* (1987), and *A Raisin in the Sun* (2004), for which she became the first African American actress to win the Tony Award for Best Actress in a Play.

ANN REINKING was a dancer, choreographer, and director. She was a four-time Tony Award nominee, winning for her Fosse-inspired choreography for *Chicago* (1996).

ALFONSO RIBEIRO made his Broadway debut in the title role in *The Tap Dance Kid* (1983) before turning to film and TV, including *The Fresh Prince of Bel-Air*.

CHITA RIVERA is a ten-time Tony Award nominee and a two-time winner, for *The Rink* (1984) and *Kiss of the Spider Woman* (1993). Her career has spanned seven decades and includes performances in landmark shows such as *West Side Story* (1957), *Bye Bye Birdie* (1960), and *Chicago* (1975). She was awarded a Special Tony Award for Lifetime Achievement in 2018.

JEROME ROBBINS was a director and choreographer in ballet, theater, and film, who helmed such iconic shows as *On the Town* (1944), *The King and I* (1951), *West Side Story* (1957), *Gypsy* (1959), and *Fiddler on the Roof* (1964). He was a founding choreographer of New York City Ballet and the recipient of five Tony Awards, two Academy Awards, a Kennedy Center Honor, and the National Medal of Arts.

RICHARD RODGERS was an Emmy, Grammy, Oscar, Tony, and Pulitzer-winning composer best known for his work as part of two legendary duos, including *On Your Toes* (1936), *The Boys from Syracuse* (1938), and *Pal Joey* (1940) with Lorenz Hart, and *Oklahoma!* (1943), *Carousel* (1945), *South Pacific* (1949), *The King and I* (1951), and *The Sound of Music* (1959) with Oscar Hammerstein II. He was also a Kennedy Center Honoree.

DAPHNE RUBIN-VEGA is a two-time Tony Award nominee, for Best Actress in a Musical for her Broadway debut as Mimi in *Rent* (1996) and for Best Featured Actress in a Play for *Anna in the Tropics* (2003).

NEIL SIMON received more combined Oscar and Tony nominations than any other writer. He won Tony Awards for *The Odd Couple* (1965), *Biloxi Blues* (1985), and *Lost in Yonkers* (1991), for which he also won a Pulitzer Prize, plus a Special Tony for "Contribution to the Theatre." In 1983, the Alvin Theatre was renamed the Neil Simon Theatre in his honor, and in 1995, he was a Kennedy Center Honoree.

STEPHEN SONDHEIM is among contemporary musical theater's most acclaimed composer-lyricists. He is the winner of a Pulitzer, an Oscar, eight Grammys, and eight Tony Awards—more than any other songwriter—for shows including *Follies* (1971), *A Little Night Music* (1973), *Sweeney Todd* (1979), and *Into the Woods* (1987). He is also the recipient of a Kennedy Center Honor and the National Medal of Arts. In 2010, Broadway's Henry Miller's Theatre was renamed the Stephen Sondheim Theatre in his honor.

BARBRA STREISAND is an acclaimed recording artist, actress, and filmmaker. She originated the role of Fanny Brice in *Funny Girl* (1964) and in the 1968 film, winning an Oscar. She has won two Oscars, four Emmys, ten Grammys, and a Special Tony Award for "Star of the Decade."

ALI STROKER rose to stardom on *The Glee Project* before becoming the first actress who uses a wheelchair to appear on Broadway, in *Spring Awakening* (2015), and the first to win a Tony Award, for her turn as Ado Annie in *Oklahoma!* (2019).

SUSAN STROMAN is a fourteen-time Tony nominee and five-time winner, for her choreography work on *Crazy for You* (1992), *Show Boat* (1994), and *Contact* (2000), and for direction and choreography on *The Producers* (2001).

MICHEL STUART created the role of Greg in *A Chorus Line* (1975) before finding success as a producer of shows including *Nine* (1982), for which he won a Tony for Best Musical.

JESSICA TANDY's seven-decade career as an actress earned her four Tony Awards, including one for her performance as Blanche DuBois in *A Streetcar Named Desire* (1947) and a Special Tony for Lifetime Achievement in 1994. She won an Oscar for *Driving Miss Daisy* and an Emmy for *Foxfire*.

JEANINE TESORI is one of Broadway's most prolific and acclaimed contemporary composers. A five-time Tony Award nominee and one-time winner for *Fun Home* (2015) with lyricist Lisa Kron, she has also collaborated on *Thoroughly Modern Millie* (2002) with lyricist Dick Scanlan, *Caroline, or Change* (2004) with lyricist Tony Kushner, and *Shrek: The Musical* (2008) with lyricist David Lindsay-Abaire. She is a two-time finalist for the Pulitzer Prize for Drama.

MARY TESTA is a three-time Tony Award–nominated actress, for *On the Town* (1998), *42nd Street* (2001), and *Oklahoma!* (2019).

TOMMY TUNE is a performer, director, and choreographer, and the recipient of ten Tony Awards, including a Special Tony for Lifetime Achievement, and the National Medal of Arts. His Tony wins include Best Actor for *My One and Only* (1983) and Best Direction and Choreography for *Grand Hotel* (1989).

GWEN VERDON wowed Broadway as an actress and dancer in landmark shows including *Damn Yankees* (1955), *Sweet Charity* (1966), and *Chicago* (1975). She won four Tony Awards.

ROBIN WAGNER is a three-time Tony Award–winning scenic designer whose many credits include *Hair* (1968), *A Chorus Line* (1975), *Dreamgirls* (1981), *Angels in America* (1993), and *The Producers* (2001).

THOMMIE WALSH originated the role of Bobby in *A Chorus Line* (1975) before turning to a career in choreography. He won two Tony Awards with collaborator Tommy Tune for *A Day in Hollywood / A Night in the Ukraine* (1980) and *My One and Only* (1983).

WENDY WASSERSTEIN was a writer, playwright, and screenwriter whose best-known play, *The Heidi Chronicles* (1989), won the Tony Award for Best Play and the Pulitzer Prize for Drama. She also received a Tony nomination for *The Sisters Rosensweig* (1993).

ETHEL WATERS broke down racial barriers on Broadway and beyond, appearing in the revues *Africana* (1927) and *As Thousands Cheer* (1933) at a time when the stage and screen offered limited access to Black performers. She was the second Black actress to be nominated for an Academy Award and the first to be nominated for an Emmy.

ANDREW LLOYD WEBBER is an Emmy, Grammy, Oscar, and Tony-winning composer whose Broadway and West End hits include *Jesus Christ Superstar* (1971), *Evita* (1979), *Joseph and the Amazing Technicolor Dreamcoat* (1982), *Cats* (1982), *The Phantom of the Opera* (1988), and *Sunset Boulevard* (1994). He is also the recipient of a Kennedy Center Honor.

SAMMY WILLIAMS won the Tony Award for Best Featured Actor in a Musical for his heartbreaking turn as Paul in *A Chorus Line* (1975).

TENNESSEE WILLIAMS, one of the foremost twentieth-century American playwrights, wrote acclaimed dramas including *The Glass Menagerie* (1945) and *The Rose Tattoo* (1951), for which he won his sole Tony Award, as well as *A Streetcar Named Desire* (1947) and *Cat on a Hot Tin Roof* (1955), both of which won Pulitzer Prizes.

AUGUST WILSON was a playwright whose work chronicled the African American experience, including *Ma Rainey's Black Bottom* (1984); *Fences* (1987), which won him both a Tony Award and a Pulitzer Prize; and *The Piano Lesson* (1990), for which he won a second Pulitzer. After his death in 2005, the Virginia Theatre was renamed the August Wilson Theatre in his honor.

MARISSA JARET WINOKUR appeared in *Grease* (1994) on Broadway before creating the role of Tracy Turnblad in *Hairspray* (2002), for which she won the Tony Award for Best Actress in a Musical.

GEORGE C. WOLFE is a director, producer, and writer whose Broadway credits as director include *Angels in America* (1993) and *Bring in 'da Noise, Bring in 'da Funk* (1996), both of which earned him Tony Awards. He was Artistic Director of The Public Theater from 1993 until 2004.

DEBORAH YATES was nominated for the Tony Award for Best Featured Actress in a Musical for her performance as the iconic Girl in a Yellow Dress in *Contact* (2000).

FLORENZ ZIEGFELD, JR., produced dozens of Broadway shows in the late nineteenth and early twentieth centuries, including the star-studded revues *The Ziegfeld Follies* and the premiere production of *Show Boat* (1927).

For my Aunt Martha, the Mame to my Patrick —J.R.A.

To Joe Allen, who did more for Broadway without ever stepping on a stage —P.E.

Text copyright © 2021 by John Robert Allman

Jacket art and interior illustrations copyright © 2021 by Peter Emmerich

All rights reserved. Published in the United States by Doubleday, an imprint of Random House Children's Books, a division of Penguin Random House LLC, New York.

Doubleday and the colophon are registered trademarks of Penguin Random House LLC.

Playbill trademark used by permission. All rights reserved, Playbill Inc.

Visit us on the Web! rhcbooks.com

Educators and librarians, for a variety of teaching tools, visit us at RHTeachersLibrarians.com

Library of Congress Cataloging-in-Publication Data is available upon request.

ISBN 978-0-593-30563-8 (trade) — ISBN 978-0-593-30565-2 (ebook)

MANUFACTURED IN CHINA

10 9 8 7 6 5 4 3 2 1

First Edition

Autographs